"Making Money with Social Media: A Step-by-Step Guide"

Introduction

Welcome to "Making Money with Social Media: A Step-by-Step Guide," your indispensable companion on the journey to unlocking the full financial potential of your online presence. In the ever-evolving digital landscape, social media has become more than a platform for connection; it's a gateway to financial opportunity. Tailored for the all audience, this guide provides a comprehensive and practical roadmap for individuals and businesses alike.

As we navigate the intricacies of social media, we embark on a step-by-step exploration of proven strategies to transform your online activities into sustainable revenue streams. From leveraging affiliate marketing to creating compelling sponsored content, and from selling products or services to exploring innovative monetization avenues, each chapter is a strategic building block towards financial success.

This guide goes beyond generic advice, offering tailored insights for navigating the social media landscape. Whether you're an aspiring influencer, a content creator, or a business owner seeking to maximize your online reach, you'll find actionable tips, real-world examples, and expert guidance to propel you towards financial empowerment.

Embrace the transformative power of social media not just as a means of communication, but as a dynamic platform for generating income. With this step-by-step guide, you're not just navigating the digital realm; you're charting a course towards financial independence and success in the vibrant world of social media. Let's embark on this journey together and turn your social media presence into a thriving source of income.

Index

1. **Affiliate Marketing Mastery:** Learn the art of affiliate marketing, harnessing the power of partnerships to earn commissions through product recommendations.
2. **Sponsored Posts Savvy:** Navigate the world of sponsored content creation, transforming your social media presence into a platform for brand collaborations and endorsements.
3. **Product Sales Prowess:** Master the nuances of selling products or services directly through your social media channels, creating seamless and lucrative transactions.
4. **Brand Ambassadorship:** Embrace brand ambassadorship as a strategic collaboration, establishing long-term relationships with brands that align with your personal or business ethos.
5. **Coaching and Consultancy:** Offer your expertise through coaching or consultancy services, leveraging your social media influence to attract clients seeking your unique insights.
6. **Crowdfunding for Creatives:** Explore crowdfunding options to fund your creative projects, turning your social media following into a supportive community.
7. **Digital Products Delight:** Create and sell digital products, from e-books to online courses, expanding your revenue streams beyond traditional avenues.
8. **Freelancing Freedom:** Leverage your social media presence to attract freelance opportunities, showcasing your skills and expertise to a wider audience.
9. **YouTube Ad Revenue:** Uncover the strategies for earning through YouTube ad revenue, capitalizing on the vast audience of this video-sharing platform.

10. **Webinar Wealth:** Host webinars to share your knowledge and insights, monetizing your expertise and engaging with a captivated online audience.
11. **Strategic Stock Photography:** Turn your photography skills into a revenue stream by selling stock images through social media platforms or dedicated websites.
12. **Podcasting Profits:** Venture into podcasting, exploring avenues such as sponsorships, ads, and listener-supported funding for a diversified income stream.
13. **Influencer Events Income:** Organize or participate in influencer events, creating opportunities for networking, collaborations, and potential revenue generation.
14. **Sponsored Webinars and Takeovers:** Elevate your brand visibility by offering sponsored webinars or takeovers, providing value to your audience while partnering with relevant brands.
15. **Merchandise Magic:** Capitalize on your brand by selling merchandise, from branded apparel to accessories, enhancing your revenue while strengthening your brand presence.

Embark on a transformative journey through these 15 ways, each offering a unique pathway to monetizing your social media presence. With this step-by-step guide, you'll navigate the British social media landscape with confidence, turning your online activities into a thriving source of income.

Chapter 1

Affiliate Marketing Mastery:

Unveiling the Secrets to Digital Revenue Success

In the intricate web of online commerce, mastering the art of Affiliate Marketing emerges as a pivotal strategy for individuals and businesses seeking to harness the potential of digital partnerships. This comprehensive guide dives deep into the nuances of Affiliate Marketing Mastery, offering a roadmap for success in the dynamic landscape of e-commerce.

Understanding the Essence of Affiliate Marketing:

Affiliate Marketing is more than a transactional strategy; it's a collaborative dance between content creators and brands. At its core, it involves promoting products or services and earning a commission for every sale generated through the affiliate's unique link. However, Affiliate Marketing Mastery transcends the basics, focusing on strategic approaches to maximize earnings and build sustainable relationships.

Crafting Compelling Content:

Central to Affiliate Marketing Mastery is the ability to create content that resonates with the target audience. Successful affiliates understand the importance of authenticity, weaving product recommendations seamlessly into their narrative. Whether through blog posts, videos, or social media updates, the art lies in blending promotional content with valuable information, establishing trust with followers.

Choosing Profitable Niches and Products:

Affiliate Marketing Mastery begins with strategic niche selection. Identifying a niche that aligns with your interests, expertise, and audience preferences is crucial. Equally important is the selection of high-quality, reputable products or services to promote. The choice of products should resonate with your audience, adding value to their lives and reinforcing your credibility as an affiliate.

Building a Robust Affiliate Strategy:

Affiliate Marketing is not a one-size-fits-all endeavor. Mastery comes through the development of a personalized and strategic approach. Successful affiliates diversify their promotional methods, combining various channels such as blog content, social media, email marketing, and even webinars to reach a broader audience. A comprehensive strategy also involves tracking performance metrics, understanding what works, and adapting strategies accordingly.

Navigating Affiliate Networks:

Affiliate Marketing Mastery necessitates an understanding of affiliate networks. These networks act as intermediaries connecting affiliates with a myriad of brands. Choosing the right affiliate network involves assessing factors such as commission structures, payment reliability, and the availability of products relevant to your niche. Mastery lies in forging partnerships with reputable brands and understanding the terms of engagement.

Building Trust with Your Audience:

Trust is the currency of Affiliate Marketing Mastery. Influential affiliates focus on building genuine relationships with their audience. They disclose affiliations transparently, share honest reviews, and prioritize the interests of their followers. Building a reputation as a trustworthy source enhances the effectiveness of affiliate promotions and fosters long-term audience loyalty.

Optimizing for Conversions:

Beyond mere promotion, Affiliate Marketing Mastery involves a keen understanding of conversion optimization. From strategic placement of affiliate links to crafting compelling calls-to-action, successful affiliates continually refine their approach to enhance conversion rates. A mastery of analytics tools is crucial for assessing which strategies yield the best results.

Staying Compliant with Regulations:

Affiliate Marketing Mastery requires an awareness of legal and ethical considerations. Affiliates must comply with advertising regulations, disclose their relationships with brands clearly, and ensure transparency in promotional efforts. Staying informed about industry guidelines prevents potential legal issues and protects both affiliates and their audiences.

Monetizing Affiliate Marketing Mastery:

Ultimately, the goal of Affiliate Marketing Mastery is to transform promotional efforts into tangible revenue. Successful affiliates explore innovative ways to monetize their expertise, such as negotiating higher commission rates, creating bonus offers for their audience, and even negotiating exclusive deals with partner brands.

In conclusion, Affiliate Marketing Mastery is a multifaceted journey that goes beyond the basics. It involves strategic content creation, thoughtful selection of products and niches, building trust with audiences, and optimizing for conversions. With this guide, aspiring affiliates can navigate the intricacies of the affiliate marketing landscape, unlocking the potential for sustainable and lucrative digital revenue.

Chapter 2

Sponsored Posts Savvy:

Navigating the Landscape of Influencer Marketing

In the dynamic realm of digital influence, mastering the art of Sponsored Posts represents a pivotal strategy for individuals and brands seeking to harness the potential of influencer marketing. This comprehensive guide delves into the essence of Sponsored Posts Savvy, offering insights into the intricacies of crafting compelling content, fostering collaborations, and maximizing the transformative impact on both influencers and their partnering brands.

Understanding the Dynamics of Sponsored Posts:

At its core, Sponsored Posts involve influencers collaborating with brands to create content that seamlessly integrates promotional messaging. It's a delicate balance between authentic storytelling and brand representation. Sponsored Posts Savvy goes beyond mere promotion; it's about creating a narrative that resonates with the audience while effectively showcasing the partner brand.

The Art of Authentic Storytelling:

Successful Sponsored Posts Savvy hinges on the ability to tell authentic stories. Influencers who master this art integrate brand messages organically into their content, ensuring a seamless flow that resonates with their audience. Authenticity builds trust, and in the world of influencer marketing, trust is the currency that enhances the effectiveness of Sponsored Posts.

Selecting Relevant Brand Collaborations:

The journey to Sponsored Posts Savvy commences with strategic collaboration selection. Influencers must align with brands that complement their niche, values, and audience demographics. The synergy between influencer and brand enhances the authenticity of the sponsored content, creating a natural fit that resonates with followers.

Navigating Brand Guidelines and Creativity:

While Sponsored Posts follow brand guidelines, Savvy influencers infuse creativity into their content. It's about finding the perfect balance between adhering to brand expectations and injecting a personal touch that reflects the influencer's unique style. This delicate dance between guidelines and creativity ensures that the content feels genuine and engaging.

Fostering Long-Term Relationships:

Beyond individual Sponsored Posts, Savvy influencers understand the value of fostering long-term relationships with brands. Consistent collaboration builds a narrative thread, reinforcing brand association and establishing a deeper connection with the audience. This approach transforms sporadic promotions into a cohesive brand journey.

Leveraging Diverse Content Formats:

Sponsored Posts Savvy encompasses an understanding of diverse content formats. Whether through captivating visuals, engaging videos, or insightful blog posts, influencers leverage different mediums to convey brand messages effectively. This adaptability ensures that the sponsored content aligns with the preferences of the influencer's audience.

Quantifying Impact and Engagement:

Mastery in Sponsored Posts involves more than just creating aesthetically pleasing content. Savvy influencers employ analytics tools to quantify the impact and engagement generated by sponsored collaborations. By understanding metrics such as reach, impressions, and audience engagement, influencers refine their strategies for future campaigns.

Ethical Considerations and Transparency:

Sponsored Posts Savvy prioritizes ethical considerations and transparency. Influencers openly disclose their partnerships, ensuring that their audience is aware of any promotional collaborations. This transparency builds trust and credibility, fostering an environment where sponsored content is viewed as a genuine recommendation rather than mere advertising.

Monetizing Sponsored Posts Expertise:

As influencers ascend to Sponsored Posts Savvy, they explore avenues for monetizing their expertise. Negotiating fair compensation, securing long-term partnerships, and even offering additional promotional services become part of the influencer's repertoire, transforming sponsored collaborations into a sustainable source of income.

In conclusion, Sponsored Posts Savvy is a multifaceted journey that blends authenticity, strategic collaboration, and creativity. It's about more than showcasing products or services; it's about creating a narrative that captivates audiences while effectively conveying brand messages. This guide equips influencers with the insights to navigate the landscape of sponsored content, ensuring that each collaboration is not just a promotional opportunity but a meaningful and impactful storytelling experience.

Chapter 3

Product Sales Prowess:

Mastering the Art of Selling in the Digital Landscape

In the fast-evolving landscape of digital commerce, the quest for Product Sales Prowess has become a paramount pursuit for individuals and businesses alike. This comprehensive guide delves into the intricacies of mastering the art of selling products in the digital realm, offering insights into strategic planning, online storefront creation, marketing tactics, and the transformative impact on both sellers and consumers in the British market.

Crafting a Strategic Sales Plan:

Product Sales Prowess begins with meticulous strategic planning. Sellers must define their target audience, understand market trends, and identify unique selling propositions. A well-crafted sales plan provides a roadmap for product positioning, pricing strategies, and avenues for online visibility.

Establishing a Robust Online Storefront:

The heart of Product Sales Prowess lies in the creation of a robust online storefront. Whether through dedicated websites, e-commerce platforms, or social media marketplaces, sellers must create a seamless and visually appealing shopping experience. Customisation, user-friendly interfaces, and secure payment gateways are essential elements in fostering consumer trust.

Leveraging Digital Marketing Strategies:

Mastering the art of selling involves a deep understanding of digital marketing strategies. From search engine optimisation (SEO) to social media advertising, successful sellers employ a multi-channel approach. Content marketing, influencer collaborations, and email campaigns play pivotal roles in driving traffic and converting leads into customers.

Creating Compelling Product Descriptions and Visuals:

Product Sales Prowess requires the ability to communicate the value of products effectively. Sellers must craft compelling product descriptions that highlight features, benefits, and unique selling points. High-quality visuals, including images and videos, enhance the overall presentation and provide potential buyers with a closer look at the products.

Optimizing for User Experience:

Seamless user experience is a cornerstone of successful product sales. Sellers must optimize their online platforms for easy navigation, quick load times, and mobile responsiveness. A positive user experience contributes to customer satisfaction and encourages repeat business.

Implementing Secure and Convenient Payment Options:

Providing secure and convenient payment options is a non-negotiable aspect of Product Sales Prowess. Sellers should offer a variety of payment methods, ensuring that customers can choose the option that suits them best. Additionally, integrating trusted payment gateways reinforces the credibility of the online storefront.

Building Customer Trust through Reviews and Testimonials:

Trust is paramount in the digital marketplace. Product Sales Prowess involves actively seeking and displaying customer reviews and testimonials. Positive feedback builds credibility, addresses potential buyer concerns, and influences purchasing decisions.

Strategising Pricing Models:

Successful sellers understand the nuances of pricing strategies. Whether employing competitive pricing, value-based pricing, or bundling options, the chosen pricing model should align with market dynamics while providing perceived value to customers.

Implementing Customer Retention Strategies:

Product Sales Prowess extends beyond the initial transaction. Sellers should implement customer retention strategies such as loyalty programs, personalized offers, and post-purchase engagement. Building lasting relationships with customers contributes to long-term success.

Navigating Legal and Regulatory Considerations:

Sellers must be well-versed in legal and regulatory considerations. Compliance with consumer protection laws, data privacy regulations, and e-commerce guidelines is essential. Navigating these considerations ensures a smooth and ethical selling process.

Monetising Expertise through Upselling and Cross-selling:

Beyond individual transactions, Product Sales Prowess involves upselling and cross-selling. Sellers leverage their expertise to recommend complementary products or premium versions, increasing the average transaction value and maximizing revenue.

Utilizing Limited-Time Offers and Promotions:

Strategic use of limited-time offers and promotions is a hallmark of Product Sales Prowess. Sellers create a sense of urgency, encouraging buyers to take immediate action. Well-timed promotions contribute to increased sales and heightened consumer engagement.

Adapting to Market Trends and Innovations:

Remaining at the forefront of market trends and technological innovations is essential for Product Sales Prowess. Sellers should embrace emerging technologies, explore new sales channels, and stay agile in response to evolving consumer preferences.

Measuring and Analyzing Key Performance Indicators (KPIs):

To refine and optimize their strategies, sellers must continually measure and analyze key performance indicators (KPIs). From conversion rates to customer acquisition costs, data-driven insights guide decision-making and enhance overall sales performance.

Cultivating a Brand Persona:

Product Sales Prowess goes beyond individual transactions; it involves cultivating a brand persona. Successful sellers curate a distinctive brand identity, fostering an emotional connection with consumers that extends beyond products to a lifestyle or ethos.

In conclusion, Product Sales Prowess is a dynamic and multifaceted journey that combines strategic planning, technological proficiency, and customer-centric approaches. As sellers master the art of digital commerce, they not only drive sales but also shape positive consumer experiences, contributing to long-term success in the competitive world of online selling. This guide equips sellers with the knowledge and strategies to navigate the digital marketplace with confidence, transforming their online storefronts into thriving hubs of Product Sales Prowess.

Chapter 4

Brand Ambassadorship:

Nurturing Authentic Connections in the Digital Landscape

In the ever-evolving realm of digital influence, Brand Ambassadorship emerges as a powerful strategy, transcending traditional marketing approaches. This comprehensive guide navigates the intricacies of

Brand Ambassadorship, delving into the essence of authentic connections, strategic partnerships, and the transformative impact on both ambassadors and the brands they represent.

Defining Brand Ambassadorship:

Brand Ambassadorship is more than a contractual arrangement; it's a symbiotic relationship between individuals and brands. Ambassadors embody the ethos, values, and personality of a brand, fostering a genuine connection with their audience while actively promoting and endorsing products or services.

Fostering Authentic Relationships:

At the core of Brand Ambassadorship is the cultivation of authentic relationships. Successful ambassadors go beyond scripted endorsements, integrating brand messaging seamlessly into their lifestyle and narrative. Authenticity builds trust, transforming promotional content into relatable and genuine recommendations.

Strategic Alignment between Ambassador and Brand:

Brand Ambassadorship flourishes when there is strategic alignment between the ambassador and the brand. Ambassadors carefully select partnerships that resonate with their personal brand, ensuring a natural fit that enhances credibility and resonates with their audience.

Building Long-Term Brand Narratives:

The essence of Brand Ambassadorship lies in building long-term brand narratives. Ambassadors become storytellers, weaving a cohesive and engaging narrative around the brand. This continuity contributes to a deeper connection with the audience, creating a consistent brand experience.

Leveraging Diverse Platforms for Engagement:

Ambassadors are adept at leveraging diverse platforms to engage with their audience. From social media platforms to blogs and events, successful Brand Ambassadorship involves a strategic multichannel approach. Ambassadors create an omnipresence that extends the brand's reach across various digital touchpoints.

Navigating Ethical and Transparent Practices:

Ethical considerations are paramount in Brand Ambassadorship. Transparency regarding the ambassador's relationship with the brand is crucial. Ambassadors openly disclose their affiliations, maintaining the trust of their audience and adhering to industry guidelines and regulations.

Measuring Impact through Analytics:

Quantifying the impact of Brand Ambassadorship involves leveraging analytics tools. From tracking engagement metrics to monitoring the growth of brand-specific KPIs, ambassadors use data-driven insights to demonstrate the tangible impact of their efforts.

Monetizing Ambassadorship Expertise:

Brand Ambassadorship extends beyond promotional efforts; successful ambassadors monetize their expertise. Negotiating fair compensation, securing exclusive deals, and exploring additional revenue streams become integral components of the ambassador's skill set.

Cultivating a Personal Brand:

Brand Ambassadorship often aligns with the cultivation of a personal brand. Ambassadors become influencers in their own right, with a distinct voice and identity. This dual-branding approach enhances the ambassador's marketability and influence.

Long-Term Loyalty and Advocacy:

The pinnacle of successful Brand Ambassadorship is the cultivation of long-term loyalty and advocacy. Ambassadors evolve into brand advocates, fostering a sense of loyalty that extends beyond contractual obligations. This advocacy transforms customers into brand enthusiasts, contributing to sustained success.

Navigating Challenges and Controversies:

Brand Ambassadorship isn't immune to challenges. Ambassadors may face controversies or changing brand priorities. Navigating these challenges requires adaptability, effective communication, and a commitment to upholding the integrity of the brand.

Global Impact and Cultural Sensitivity:

In the digital age, Brand Ambassadorship often transcends geographical boundaries. Ambassadors navigate the nuances of global impact, ensuring cultural sensitivity in their endorsements. A global approach broadens the brand's appeal and resonates with diverse audiences.

Inclusive Representation and Diversity:

Brand Ambassadorship thrives on inclusive representation. Successful ambassadors champion diversity, ensuring that their endorsements reflect a broad spectrum of voices and experiences. This commitment to inclusivity enhances brand authenticity and appeal.

Environmental and Social Responsibility:

Brand Ambassadorship in the modern era is intertwined with environmental and social responsibility. Ambassadors align with brands committed to sustainability and social impact, contributing to a positive brand image and resonating with socially conscious audiences.

In conclusion, Brand Ambassadorship is a dynamic and multifaceted journey that involves more than promotional content; it's about cultivating authentic connections, building narratives, and fostering long-term loyalty. This guide equips both aspiring and established ambassadors with the insights and strategies to navigate the complexities of Brand Ambassadorship successfully, ensuring that each endorsement is a meaningful contribution to the brand's narrative and impact in the digital landscape.

Chapter 5

Coaching and Consultancy:

Guiding Success in the British Business Landscape

In the ever-evolving world of professional development and business strategy, Coaching and Consultancy have emerged as indispensable pillars for individuals and organizations seeking guidance and growth. This comprehensive guide delves into the intricacies of Coaching and Consultancy, exploring the nuanced art of mentorship, strategic advice, and the transformative impact on both clients and consultants within the unique context of the British business landscape.

Defining Coaching and Consultancy: Coaching involves a personalized and goal-oriented approach, focusing on unlocking an individual's potential, fostering skill development, and facilitating self-discovery. On the other hand, Consultancy delves into strategic problem-solving and expert advice, leveraging industry insights to guide businesses towards effective decision-making and success.

Tailoring Strategies for British Businesses: In the British business arena, Coaching and Consultancy strategies require a nuanced understanding of local markets, cultural nuances, and industry dynamics. Successful coaches and consultants tailor their approaches to align with the unique challenges and opportunities presented by the British business landscape.

Personalized Coaching for Professional Growth: Coaching, at its core, is a collaborative and personalized journey. Coaches work closely with individuals, helping them identify and achieve their professional goals. Whether refining leadership skills, navigating career transitions, or enhancing interpersonal dynamics, personalized coaching fosters holistic professional growth.

Strategic Consultancy for Business Advancement: Consultancy, on the other hand, entails a strategic partnership between consultants and businesses. Consultants bring a wealth of industry knowledge and expertise, guiding businesses through challenges, opportunities, and strategic decisions. Strategic consultancy is instrumental in enhancing operational efficiency, driving innovation, and ensuring sustainable growth.

Embracing Holistic Development: Coaching and Consultancy, when seamlessly integrated, create a holistic development approach. Personalized coaching enhances the skills and leadership capabilities of individuals, while strategic consultancy aligns organizational goals with industry best practices, fostering a comprehensive approach to success.

Cultivating Effective Communication: Effective communication is a linchpin in the success of Coaching and Consultancy. Coaches adeptly facilitate open and honest communication, creating a safe space for clients to explore challenges and opportunities. Consultants, in turn, excel in articulating complex strategies and recommendations in a clear and comprehensible manner for businesses.

Utilizing Technological Advancements: In the contemporary British business landscape, Coaching and Consultancy leverage technological advancements. Virtual coaching sessions, online consultancy platforms, and digital tools enhance accessibility and facilitate seamless collaboration, overcoming geographical constraints and ensuring timely support.

Measuring Success through Tangible Outcomes: Success in Coaching and Consultancy is measured through tangible outcomes. Coaches gauge success by the positive transformations in their clients' professional lives, while consultants assess their impact based on improved business performance, enhanced profitability, and the successful implementation of strategic initiatives.

Continuous Professional Development: For both coaches and consultants, a commitment to continuous professional development is essential. Staying abreast of industry trends, honing coaching or consultancy skills, and adopting innovative approaches ensure ongoing relevance and effectiveness in a dynamic business environment.

Navigating Ethical Considerations: Coaching and Consultancy necessitate adherence to ethical considerations. Coaches maintain confidentiality, respect client autonomy, and uphold professional boundaries. Consultants, in turn, operate with integrity, ensuring that their recommendations align with the best interests of the businesses they advise.

Cultivating a Feedback Culture: A fundamental aspect of Coaching and Consultancy is cultivating a feedback culture. Coaches provide constructive feedback to facilitate growth, while consultants seek input from clients to refine strategies and ensure alignment with evolving business needs.

Embracing Diversity and Inclusion: In the spirit of contemporary business values, successful Coaching and Consultancy embrace diversity and inclusion. Coaches champion diverse perspectives, tailoring their approaches to individuals' unique backgrounds, while consultants advocate for inclusive strategies that cater to diverse markets and audiences.

Environmental and Social Responsibility: Both Coaching and Consultancy increasingly intertwine with environmental and social responsibility. Coaches guide individuals towards leadership grounded in ethical practices, while consultants advise businesses on sustainable and socially responsible strategies, aligning with evolving societal expectations.

In conclusion, Coaching and Consultancy stand as pillars of professional development and business strategy, offering tailored guidance for individuals and organizations navigating the complexities of the British business landscape. This guide equips coaches, consultants, and those seeking their services with insights to foster growth, innovation, and success in the dynamic and diverse realm of the business arena.

Chapter 6

Crowdfunding for Creatives:

A Blueprint for Artistic Success

In the vibrant realm of creative pursuits, the power of Crowdfunding emerges as a transformative force, enabling artists, innovators, and visionaries to bring their projects to life. This comprehensive guide, "Crowdfunding for Creatives," explores the intricacies of this funding approach, providing a blueprint for artistic success in the digital age. Tailored for the creative minds seeking to turn their dreams into reality, this guide navigates the landscape of crowdfunding with a focus on unleashing artistic potential, engaging communities, and crafting compelling campaigns.

Demystifying Crowdfunding: At its essence, Crowdfunding for Creatives demystifies the crowdfunding process. It breaks down the steps involved, from conceptualizing a campaign to navigating crowdfunding platforms, empowering creatives to overcome financial barriers and turn their passion projects into tangible realities.

Navigating Platform Selection: Choosing the right crowdfunding platform is a crucial step in the creative journey. This guide offers insights into the diverse platforms available, helping creatives match their projects with the platform that aligns best with their artistic goals and target audience.

Crafting Compelling Campaigns: Success in crowdfunding hinges on the ability to craft compelling campaigns. Creatives learn the art of storytelling, conveying the essence of their projects in a way that resonates with potential backers. From engaging videos to captivating project descriptions, this guide provides strategies to capture the imaginations of backers.

Building Community Engagement: Crowdfunding for Creatives underscores the importance of community engagement. Creatives are guided in cultivating a supportive community around their projects, fostering a sense of shared enthusiasm and dedication. Strategies for leveraging social media, email newsletters, and other channels are explored to maximize audience outreach.

Setting Realistic Funding Goals: A pivotal aspect of crowdfunding success lies in setting realistic funding goals. Creatives learn to assess project needs accurately, breaking down costs and establishing transparent funding objectives. Realistic goals contribute to backer trust and confidence in the creative's ability to deliver.

Offering Irresistible Rewards: Backers are enticed not only by the creative project but also by the rewards offered. "Crowdfunding for Creatives" delves into the art of crafting irresistible rewards, aligning them with backers' interests and ensuring they complement the overall project experience.

Navigating the Rewards Fulfillment Process: Successful crowdfunding extends beyond funding attainment to the seamless fulfillment of rewards. Creatives receive guidance on planning and executing the rewards fulfillment process, ensuring backers feel valued and appreciated for their support.

Maintaining Transparency and Communication: Transparency is paramount in the world of crowdfunding. Creatives are coached on maintaining open and honest communication with backers throughout the campaign and beyond. Regular updates, progress reports, and addressing challenges transparently build trust and goodwill.

Post-Campaign Strategies: "Crowdfunding for Creatives" extends its guidance into the post-campaign phase. Creatives learn strategies for keeping backers engaged, expressing gratitude, and effectively transitioning from crowdfunding success to project realization.

Mitigating Challenges and Overcoming Setbacks: Challenges are inevitable in any creative venture. This guide equips creatives with strategies for anticipating and mitigating challenges, providing insights into how to navigate setbacks and keep projects on track.

Navigating Legal and Ethical Considerations: Navigating the legal and ethical landscape of crowdfunding is crucial. Creatives are provided with an understanding of legal considerations, ethical responsibilities, and best practices to ensure a smooth and ethical crowdfunding journey.

Embracing Diverse Creative Projects: "Crowdfunding for Creatives" celebrates the diversity of creative projects. Whether in the realms of art, film, literature, music, or technology, this guide offers insights that can be applied universally, making it a valuable resource for creators across diverse creative disciplines.

Cultivating a Lasting Creative Community: Beyond individual campaigns, this guide emphasizes the importance of cultivating a lasting creative community. Creatives learn how to leverage their crowdfunding experiences to build an enduring network of supporters who continue to champion their artistic endeavors.

In conclusion, "Crowdfunding for Creatives" is a comprehensive and empowering guide for artists and creatives seeking to turn their imaginative projects into reality. Through strategic insights, practical tips, and a focus on community engagement, this guide serves as a valuable companion in the crowdfunding journey, unlocking the full potential of creative aspirations in the digital age.

Chapter 7

Digital Products Delight:

Crafting and Selling Irresistible Online Offerings

In the ever-evolving landscape of online commerce, the creation and sale of digital products have become a cornerstone for entrepreneurs and content creators seeking to unlock new revenue streams. "Digital Products Delight," a comprehensive guide, navigates the intricate terrain of crafting, marketing, and selling digital products with a focus on providing a delightful experience for both creators and consumers. Tailored for the digital entrepreneurs of today, this guide explores the art of digital product creation, strategic marketing, and the cultivation of a satisfied and engaged customer base.

Unleashing Creative Potential: At its core, "Digital Products Delight" is a catalyst for unleashing creative potential. It guides creators in identifying their unique skills, knowledge, and expertise that can be transformed into valuable digital products. From e-books and online courses to software and downloadable resources, this guide empowers creators to explore diverse avenues for transforming their skills into marketable digital offerings.

Crafting High-Quality Digital Products: Success in the digital marketplace hinges on the creation of high-quality products. This guide delves into the intricacies of crafting digital products that not only meet but exceed customer expectations. From design aesthetics to user experience, creators are equipped with insights to ensure their digital products are not just functional but delightful to use.

Navigating the Digital Product Landscape: The digital product landscape is diverse, and "Digital Products Delight" serves as a compass for navigating this terrain. Whether creators are delving into the world of e-commerce, mobile applications, or online subscriptions, this guide provides strategic insights tailored to the specific challenges and opportunities within each digital product category.

Strategic Pricing and Monetization: Understanding the nuances of pricing and monetization is critical in the digital space. Creators learn how to strategically price their digital products, considering factors such as perceived value, market demand, and competitive analysis. The guide also explores diverse monetization models, empowering creators to choose approaches that align with their goals and customer preferences.

Effective Digital Marketing Strategies: The journey from creation to sales involves effective digital marketing. "Digital Products Delight" explores proven strategies for marketing digital products across various online channels. From content marketing and social media promotion to email campaigns, creators gain insights into building awareness, driving traffic, and converting potential customers into delighted buyers.

Building a Brand and Customer Loyalty: Digital Products Delight emphasizes the importance of building a brand identity that resonates with the target audience. Creators learn how to infuse their digital products with a distinctive brand personality, fostering customer loyalty and creating a lasting connection with their audience.

Enhancing Customer Experience: Beyond the point of purchase, the guide delves into enhancing the overall customer experience. From user-friendly interfaces to responsive customer support, creators discover strategies to ensure that every interaction with their digital products is seamless and delightful, fostering positive reviews and repeat business.

Utilizing Feedback for Iterative Improvement: Continuous improvement is a cornerstone of success in the digital product realm. Creators are guided on how to solicit and leverage customer feedback for iterative enhancements to their digital offerings. This iterative approach ensures that digital products remain relevant and aligned with evolving customer needs.

Navigating Legal and Ethical Considerations: Digital Products Delight extends its guidance to the legal and ethical considerations surrounding digital product creation and sales. Creators gain an understanding of copyright issues, licensing agreements, and privacy considerations, ensuring that their digital ventures operate within ethical and legal boundaries.

Monetizing Expertise Beyond the Product: Monetizing expertise goes beyond the initial sale. "Digital Products Delight" explores avenues for creators to leverage their expertise beyond product sales, such as offering premium content, consulting services, or exclusive memberships. This multifaceted approach enhances revenue streams and solidifies creators as authorities in their respective niches.

In conclusion, "Digital Products Delight" is a comprehensive guide for digital entrepreneurs, equipping them with the strategies, insights, and best practices to create, market, and sell digital products successfully. Whether novices exploring the digital landscape or seasoned creators looking to enhance their offerings, this guide serves as a valuable companion, ensuring that each digital product crafted becomes a source of delight for both creators and consumers in the dynamic world of online commerce.

Chapter 8

Freelancing Freedom:

Crafting Your Path to Success in the Gig Economy

In the landscape of modern work, "Freelancing Freedom" stands as a guiding light, offering a comprehensive roadmap for individuals seeking autonomy, flexibility, and prosperity in the realm of freelancing. This e-book delves into the intricacies of freelancing, equipping aspiring freelancers and seasoned professionals alike with the tools, strategies, and insights needed to navigate the gig economy and carve a fulfilling and successful freelance career.

Understanding the Gig Economy: At its core, "Freelancing Freedom" contextualizes the gig economy, elucidating its dynamics, opportunities, and challenges. It illuminates the shift from traditional employment to independent work, underscoring the value of freelancing as a viable and rewarding career choice.

Identifying Skills and Niche Specialization: Key to freelancing success is identifying one's skills and carving a niche. This e-book empowers individuals to assess their strengths, passions, and expertise, guiding them to carve a specialized niche that aligns with market demands and personal aspirations.

Navigating the Freelance Landscape: Navigating the freelance landscape requires a strategic approach. "Freelancing Freedom" provides insights into diverse freelance platforms, marketplaces, and client acquisition strategies. From building a standout portfolio to networking effectively, freelancers gain a comprehensive understanding of the multifaceted freelance terrain.

Establishing a Personal Brand: A cornerstone of freelancing success is establishing a strong personal brand. The e-book explores the art of crafting a compelling brand identity, honing a unique voice, and positioning oneself as an authority in the chosen niche. Building a personal brand fosters trust and credibility among potential clients.

Effective Client Management and Communication: Successful freelancers excel not only in their craft but also in client management and communication. "Freelancing Freedom" equips freelancers with strategies to nurture client relationships, communicate effectively, and manage expectations, ensuring a seamless and professional experience for clients.

Pricing Strategies and Negotiation Skills: Mastering pricing strategies and negotiation skills is imperative in the freelance world. This guide dives into the art of pricing services competitively, understanding market rates, and negotiating contracts that reflect the value of one's expertise, ensuring fair compensation for freelancers.

Time Management and Productivity Hacks: Freelancing often demands impeccable time management. The e-book offers practical productivity hacks, time management techniques, and strategies to maintain a work-life balance. Freelancers learn how to optimize their schedules for efficiency and productivity without compromising on personal well-being.

Managing Finances and Tax Considerations: Financial management and understanding tax considerations are pivotal for freelancers. "Freelancing Freedom" provides insights into managing finances, budgeting, invoicing, and navigating tax obligations, ensuring financial stability and compliance with regulatory requirements.

Building a Sustainable Freelance Business: Creating a sustainable freelance business is more than securing individual projects. The e-book guides freelancers in creating a long-term vision, setting goals, and diversifying income streams. It emphasizes the importance of scalability and adapting to market changes for sustainable success.

Continuous Learning and Skill Development: In the dynamic freelance landscape, continuous learning is key. "Freelancing Freedom" encourages ongoing skill development, embracing learning opportunities, and staying updated with industry trends, ensuring that freelancers remain competitive and adaptable.

Mitigating Challenges and Overcoming Setbacks: Challenges are inevitable in freelance careers. The e-book equips freelancers with strategies to anticipate and mitigate challenges, offering insights into overcoming setbacks, handling rejections, and turning obstacles into opportunities for growth.

Fostering a Supportive Freelance Community: Beyond individual pursuits, "Freelancing Freedom" emphasizes the value of a supportive freelance community. It encourages networking, collaboration, and the exchange of insights among freelancers, fostering a supportive environment for collective growth and success.

Embracing Ethical Practices and Professionalism: Ethical practices and professionalism are foundational in freelancing. The e-book underscores the importance of upholding ethical standards, maintaining integrity in client interactions, and operating with professionalism to uphold the reputation of the freelance profession.

In conclusion, "Freelancing Freedom" serves as a comprehensive guide for individuals navigating the freelance landscape. With its strategic insights, actionable advice, and focus on personal growth, this e-book empowers freelancers to craft their paths to success, achieve financial independence, and thrive in the dynamic and ever-evolving gig economy.

Chapter 9

YouTube Ad Revenue Mastery:

Monetize Your Content and Maximize Earnings

In the digital era, YouTube stands as a powerful platform where content creators can not only share their passion but also turn it into a lucrative venture. "YouTube Ad Revenue Mastery," a comprehensive e-book, unlocks the strategies and techniques essential for content creators to monetize their channels effectively and maximize earnings through YouTube's ad revenue program. Tailored for both aspiring YouTubers and established creators, this guide navigates the intricacies of the YouTube ecosystem, providing insights into content creation, audience engagement, and the optimization of ad revenue potential.

Understanding the YouTube Ad Revenue System: At the heart of "YouTube Ad Revenue Mastery" lies a deep dive into the YouTube Partner Program and the ad revenue system. Creators gain a thorough understanding of eligibility criteria, monetization policies, and the revenue-sharing model, laying the foundation for strategic monetization.

Optimizing Content for Monetization: Monetization begins with content creation. This ebook guides content creators in optimizing their videos for ad revenue. From choosing niche-relevant topics to creating engaging and high-quality content, creators learn how to attract advertisers and maximize the monetization potential of their videos.

Navigating Ad Formats and Placements: A key aspect of ad revenue mastery is understanding ad formats and placements. Creators explore the various ad types, including pre-roll, mid-roll, and display ads, learning how to strategically integrate them into their content to enhance viewer experience and increase revenue potential.

Building and Engaging Your Audience: Central to ad revenue success is building and engaging a loyal audience. The e-book provides insights into audience development strategies, fostering community engagement, and creating content that resonates with viewers. A dedicated and engaged audience is essential for maximizing ad impressions and earnings.

Leveraging YouTube Analytics for Insights: YouTube Analytics is a treasure trove of data. "YouTube Ad Revenue Mastery" equips creators with the skills to leverage analytics effectively. Creators learn how to interpret viewer demographics, analyze watch time, and identify trends, enabling them to tailor their content and optimize for higher ad revenue.

Strategic SEO Practices for Visibility: Visibility is key to attracting advertisers and increasing ad revenue. This e-book delves into strategic Search Engine Optimization (SEO) practices for YouTube. Creators discover how to optimize video titles, descriptions, and tags, ensuring their content ranks well in search results and gains maximum exposure.

Monetization Strategies Beyond Ad Revenue: While ad revenue is a significant income stream, creators are encouraged to diversify their monetization strategies. "YouTube Ad Revenue Mastery" explores alternative revenue streams, including merchandise sales, channel memberships, and sponsored content, empowering creators to build a robust and sustainable income.

Navigating Copyright and Content Policies: Monetization success requires adherence to YouTube's copyright and content policies. Creators gain insights into navigating copyright issues, avoiding content flags, and ensuring compliance with YouTube's community guidelines. A clear understanding of these policies is essential for uninterrupted ad revenue earnings.

Optimizing CPM and RPM for Higher Earnings: Creators learn the nuances of optimizing CPM (Cost Per Mille) and RPM (Revenue Per Mille) to boost earnings. The e-book provides strategies to increase ad rates, explore niche-specific advertisers, and enhance overall revenue performance, ensuring creators extract the maximum value from their content.

Effective Negotiation with Advertisers: For creators exploring sponsored content and direct ad deals, effective negotiation skills are paramount. "YouTube Ad Revenue Mastery" offers tips on negotiating with advertisers, setting fair rates, and establishing mutually beneficial partnerships that complement ad revenue earnings.

Navigating the YouTube Ad Revenue Market Trends: Staying abreast of market trends is crucial for sustained ad revenue success. Creators are guided on how to adapt to changing market dynamics, explore emerging niches, and align their content with evolving advertiser preferences to stay competitive in the ever-evolving digital landscape.

Mitigating Challenges and Adapting to Algorithm Changes: Challenges and algorithm changes are inherent in the digital realm. This ebook equips creators with strategies to navigate algorithm updates, adapt their content strategies, and mitigate challenges to maintain consistent ad revenue earnings.

Embracing Inclusivity and Diverse Content Creation: YouTube's global reach requires creators to embrace inclusivity. "YouTube Ad Revenue Mastery" emphasizes the importance of creating diverse and inclusive content that resonates with a broad audience, expanding reach, and attracting advertisers targeting diverse demographics.

In conclusion, "YouTube Ad Revenue Mastery" serves as an indispensable guide for content creators aiming to monetize their passion and maximize earnings on the YouTube platform. By navigating the complexities of ad revenue, optimizing content, and diversifying monetization strategies, creators can transform their YouTube channels into lucrative ventures, achieving financial success while continuing to engage and inspire their audience.

Chapter 10

Webinar Wealth:

Mastering the Art of Profitable Online Presentations

In the dynamic landscape of online communication, webinars have emerged as powerful tools for engagement, education, and, most importantly, revenue generation. "Webinar Wealth," a comprehensive e-book, serves as a roadmap for individuals and businesses looking to harness the potential of webinars to not only share valuable content but also create a substantial income stream. This guide navigates the intricate process of planning, promoting, and monetizing webinars, providing actionable insights for both beginners and experienced presenters seeking to unlock the full financial potential of this digital platform.

Understanding the Webinar Landscape: At its core, "Webinar Wealth" begins by demystifying the webinar landscape. It explores the various types of webinars, their purposes, and the diverse ways in which individuals and businesses can leverage this powerful communication medium. From educational seminars to product launches and sales presentations, the e-book establishes the broad spectrum of opportunities within the world of webinars.

Strategic Planning and Execution: Success in webinars hinges on meticulous planning and execution. This guide walks presenters through the strategic process of planning compelling webinar content, selecting the right format, and creating a seamless and engaging presentation. From defining objectives to structuring content for maximum impact, "Webinar Wealth" ensures that presenters are well-equipped to captivate their audience from start to finish.

Building and Engaging a Target Audience: The ebook places a significant emphasis on audience development. It provides strategies for building and engaging a target audience, ensuring that webinars reach the right individuals interested in the presented content. Techniques for leveraging social media, email marketing, and other channels are explored, enabling presenters to maximize attendance and participation.

Monetization Strategies for Webinars: "Webinar Wealth" dives into the heart of the matter—monetization. Presenters learn a myriad of strategies to turn their webinars into profitable ventures. From direct sales and product launches to premium access models and affiliate marketing, the guide provides a comprehensive toolkit for presenters to choose the most suitable monetization approach based on their content and goals.

Creating Compelling Presentation Slides and Materials: Compelling presentation materials are instrumental in the success of webinars. The e-book offers practical tips for creating visually appealing slides, handouts, and supplementary materials. Presenters learn to strike the right balance between information and engagement, ensuring that their content resonates with the audience and enhances the overall webinar experience.

Leveraging Interactive Elements: Engagement is key in a digital landscape, and "Webinar Wealth" delves into the importance of interactive elements. Presenters discover how to incorporate polls, Q&A sessions, and live chats effectively, fostering audience interaction and creating a dynamic and participatory webinar environment.

Technical Considerations and Platform Selection: Navigating the technical aspects of hosting a webinar is crucial. The e-book provides guidance on selecting the right webinar platform, ensuring technical compatibility, and troubleshooting common issues. Presenters gain insights into optimizing audio and video quality, creating a seamless and professional presentation.

Post-Webinar Strategies: The webinar journey extends beyond the live presentation. "Webinar Wealth" explores post-webinar strategies for presenters to capitalize on the momentum generated during the event. From repurposing content to nurturing post-webinar relationships, presenters learn how to extend the impact of their webinars and set the stage for future successes.

Measuring Success through Analytics: Analytics are invaluable in assessing the success of webinars. The e-book equips presenters with the knowledge to leverage analytics tools effectively. From tracking attendance and engagement metrics to analyzing conversion rates, presenters gain insights into measuring the tangible impact of their webinars and refining their strategies for future events.

Navigating Challenges and Refining Strategies: Challenges are inherent in the world of webinars, and "Webinar Wealth" prepares presenters to navigate obstacles effectively. From technical glitches to unexpected audience reactions, the guide offers strategies for overcoming challenges and adapting webinar strategies for continuous improvement.

Ethical Considerations and Transparency: Ethics and transparency are integral components of successful webinars. Presenters learn the importance of ethical considerations, including transparent disclosure of any sales or affiliate relationships. Maintaining integrity builds trust with the audience and ensures a positive reputation in the competitive webinar space.

In conclusion, "Webinar Wealth" is a comprehensive and empowering guide for individuals and businesses looking to unlock the financial potential of webinars. By providing strategic insights, practical tips, and a focus on ethical and engaging content delivery, this ebook equips presenters with the tools needed to turn their webinars into lucrative ventures, fostering both educational impact and financial success in the digital era.

Chapter 11

Strategic Stock Photography:

Crafting and Leveraging Visual Assets for Impactful Communication

In the era of digital communication, the importance of compelling visuals cannot be overstated. "Strategic Stock Photography," a comprehensive e-book, serves as a guide for individuals and businesses aiming to elevate their visual communication through strategic use of stock photography. This guide navigates the nuanced world of stock photography, providing insights into the selection, customization, and application of visual assets to enhance brand identity, captivate audiences, and drive meaningful engagement.

Understanding the Power of Visual Communication: The e-book begins by delving into the fundamental role visuals play in communication. It underscores the impact of images in conveying messages, evoking emotions, and creating memorable experiences. From website design to marketing collateral, the guide establishes the significance of visual content in the digital landscape.

Strategic Selection of Stock Photography: A key focus of "Strategic Stock Photography" is the art of selecting the right images. The guide provides strategies for aligning stock photography with brand identity, target audience preferences, and the overall communication goals. Creators and marketers learn to navigate stock photo libraries effectively, ensuring a cohesive and visually appealing representation of their brand.

Customization Techniques for Personalization: While stock photography offers a wealth of options, customization is paramount for personalization. The e-book explores techniques for customizing stock images to align with brand colors, messaging, and unique requirements. From graphic overlays to cropping and filtering, creators gain insights into making stock photos uniquely their own.

Application in Diverse Communication Channels: "Strategic Stock Photography" extends its guidance to the diverse landscape of communication channels. Whether for social media, blog posts, email marketing, or presentations, the guide provides strategies for tailoring stock photography to suit the specific requirements of each channel. Creators learn to adapt visuals for optimal impact across various platforms.

Enhancing Brand Consistency and Recognition: Brand consistency is a cornerstone of effective communication. The e-book emphasizes the role of stock photography in enhancing brand consistency. Creators discover how to curate a visual identity that resonates across all communication materials, fostering brand recognition and establishing a cohesive and memorable brand presence.

Visual Storytelling with Stock Photography: Beyond standalone visuals, the guide explores the concept of visual storytelling. Creators learn to leverage stock photography to narrate compelling stories, evoke emotions, and create a narrative thread that resonates with audiences. The power of sequential visuals in conveying a brand's journey or product evolution is explored for maximum impact.

Optimizing for Web and Mobile Platforms: In the age of digital accessibility, optimizing visuals for web and mobile platforms is essential. "Strategic Stock Photography" provides practical tips for selecting and customizing images to ensure optimal display and engagement on diverse devices. From responsive design considerations to mobile-friendly visuals, creators gain insights into reaching audiences across platforms.

Measuring Visual Impact and Engagement: Analytics play a pivotal role in refining visual strategies. The e-book equips creators with insights into measuring the impact and engagement of stock photography. Creators learn to interpret metrics related to image views, click-through rates, and social media engagement, enabling them to refine their visual strategies for ongoing effectiveness.

Legal Considerations and Ethical Use: Navigating legal and ethical considerations is integral to strategic stock photography. Creators gain an understanding of licensing agreements, copyright compliance, and ethical use of stock images. Adhering to legal standards ensures that visual content is used responsibly and mitigates the risk of legal complications.

Staying Abreast of Visual Trends: Visual trends evolve, and creators need to stay abreast of these changes. The guide explores current visual trends, equipping creators with the knowledge to select images that align with contemporary aesthetics. Staying visually relevant ensures that communication materials resonate with modern audiences.

Navigating Challenges and Overcoming Visual Hurdles: Challenges in stock photography are inevitable. "Strategic Stock Photography" prepares creators to navigate common challenges, from finding the right images amidst vast libraries to addressing visual fatigue. Strategies for overcoming hurdles ensure a seamless and efficient integration of stock photography into communication strategies.

In conclusion, "Strategic Stock Photography" serves as an invaluable resource for individuals and businesses seeking to leverage visual content for impactful communication. By providing strategic insights, customization techniques, and ethical considerations, this e-book empowers creators to harness the potential of stock photography, elevating their brand communication and fostering meaningful engagement in the visually-driven digital landscape.

Chapter 12

Podcasting Profits:

Monetizing Your Passion for Audio Excellence

In the ever-expanding realm of digital content, podcasting has emerged as a dynamic platform for creators to share stories, insights, and expertise. "Podcasting Profits," a comprehensive e-book, serves as a guide for individuals aspiring to transform their passion for audio excellence into a lucrative venture. This guide navigates the intricate landscape of podcasting, offering insights into content creation, audience engagement, and the myriad strategies for monetizing podcasts effectively.

Understanding the Podcasting Landscape: "Podcasting Profits" initiates by providing a foundational understanding of the podcasting landscape. It explores the diverse genres, formats, and potential audience demographics, setting the stage for creators to carve their niche in the expansive world of podcasting.

Strategic Content Creation for Audience Appeal: At the core of podcasting success lies compelling content creation. The e-book guides creators in strategically planning and producing podcasts that resonate with their target audience. From defining podcast themes to scripting and recording techniques, creators gain insights to captivate listeners and foster a loyal following.

Building and Engaging a Dedicated Audience: Podcasting excellence extends beyond content creation to building and engaging a dedicated audience. "Podcasting Profits" explores strategies for growing podcast audiences, leveraging social media, and fostering community engagement. Creators discover how to create a lasting connection with listeners, setting the foundation for successful monetization.

Monetization Strategies for Podcasters: A pivotal focus of the e-book is on the diverse monetization strategies available to podcasters. From traditional advertising and sponsorships to innovative approaches like listener donations, premium content subscriptions, and affiliate marketing, creators gain insights into selecting the right monetization model aligned with their content and audience.

Creating Compelling Sponsorship Proposals: Sponsorships are a cornerstone of podcast monetization. "Podcasting Profits" provides practical tips for creators to create compelling sponsorship proposals. Creators learn to communicate their podcast's value proposition effectively, attracting potential sponsors and establishing mutually beneficial partnerships that enhance their podcasting revenue.

Effective Advertising Integration: Successfully integrating advertising into podcast content requires finesse. The guide explores effective advertising strategies, ensuring that promotional content seamlessly aligns with the podcast's tone and resonates with the audience. Creators learn to strike a balance between monetization and maintaining an authentic listening experience.

Leveraging Affiliate Marketing for Additional Revenue: Affiliate marketing presents a dynamic avenue for podcast monetization. Creators discover how to strategically incorporate affiliate partnerships into their podcast content, earning commissions based on listener engagement and conversions. This approach allows creators to diversify revenue streams and maximize profitability.

Navigating Analytics for Performance Insights: Podcasting success is further enhanced by analytics insights. "Podcasting Profits" equips creators with the knowledge to navigate podcast analytics effectively. Creators learn to interpret download numbers, listener demographics, and engagement metrics, enabling them to refine their content and monetization strategies based on data-driven insights.

Optimizing for Cross-Platform Engagement: Cross-platform engagement is essential for reaching a broader audience and optimizing monetization opportunities. The guide explores strategies for expanding podcast visibility across platforms, including social media, streaming services, and podcast directories, ensuring creators maximize their reach and revenue potential.

Maintaining Consistency and Quality: Consistency and quality are paramount in podcasting. The e-book emphasizes the importance of regular content delivery, maintaining production quality, and continuously evolving to meet audience expectations. Consistency fosters audience loyalty, creating a foundation for sustained podcasting success.

Navigating Legal and Ethical Considerations: "Podcasting Profits" addresses legal and ethical considerations, ensuring creators operate within ethical boundaries and comply with copyright, licensing, and content regulations. A clear understanding of these considerations is crucial for long-term success and reputation management.

In conclusion, "Podcasting Profits" serves as a comprehensive and empowering guide for individuals seeking to monetize their passion for audio excellence. By providing strategic insights, actionable advice, and a focus on ethical and engaging content delivery, this e-book empowers podcasters to transform their podcasts into profitable ventures while maintaining the authenticity and quality that distinguishes their audio content in the competitive podcasting landscape.

Chapter 13

Influencer Events Income:

Turning Presence into Profit in the Digital Spotlight

In the dynamic realm of digital influence, the power of personal brand presence is unparalleled. "Influencer Events Income," a comprehensive e-book, serves as a guiding beacon for influencers looking to transition their online influence into tangible income through hosting and participating in events. This guide navigates the intricacies of organizing and leveraging influencer events, offering insights into strategic planning, audience engagement, and the myriad ways influencers can turn their digital spotlight into a lucrative income stream.

Understanding the Influencer Events Landscape: The e-book commences by providing an overview of the evolving landscape of influencer events. It explores the diverse types of events, ranging from virtual gatherings and webinars to in-person meetups and brand collaborations. Creators gain insights into the expansive opportunities available within the influencer events sphere.

Strategic Planning for Successful Events: At the heart of "Influencer Events Income" lies the importance of strategic event planning. Creators learn to conceptualize, plan, and execute events that align with their personal brand and resonate with their audience. From setting event goals to selecting the right format, the guide equips influencers to orchestrate events that leave a lasting impact.

Audience Engagement Strategies: In the digital age, audience engagement is a key factor in the success of influencer events. The guide explores innovative strategies for engaging audiences before, during, and after events. From social media campaigns and interactive elements to post-event follow-ups, influencers gain insights into fostering a sense of community and sustaining audience interest.

Monetization Paths for Influencer Events: Monetization is a central theme, and "Influencer Events Income" delves into various paths for influencers to generate income through events. Creators learn about ticket sales, exclusive access passes, brand sponsorships, and merchandise sales as viable avenues for turning their events into profitable ventures. The guide provides a toolkit for influencers to choose monetization strategies aligned with their brand and audience.

Crafting Compelling Event Sponsorship Proposals: Sponsorships are a key source of income for influencer events. The e-book offers practical tips for influencers to create compelling event sponsorship proposals. From showcasing the unique value of their events to articulating the benefits for sponsors, influencers gain insights into attracting lucrative partnerships that enhance the financial success of their events.

Effective Marketing and Promotion: The success of influencer events is closely tied to effective marketing and promotion. "Influencer Events Income" explores strategies for promoting events across digital channels, leveraging social media, email marketing, and other platforms to maximize reach. Creators learn to create a buzz around their events, attracting attendees and sponsors alike.

Leveraging Data and Analytics: Data and analytics play a pivotal role in refining event strategies. Creators are equipped with the knowledge to leverage data and analytics tools effectively. From tracking registration numbers to analyzing attendee demographics, influencers gain insights into measuring the success of their events and making data-driven decisions for future iterations.

Creating Memorable and Shareable Experiences: Memorable experiences are at the core of successful influencer events. The e-book guides influencers in creating experiences that resonate with attendees and are shareable across social media platforms. From interactive elements to unique event themes, influencers learn to craft experiences that leave a lasting impression and amplify their online presence.

Navigating Legal and Ethical Considerations: The guide addresses legal and ethical considerations inherent in influencer events. Creators gain an understanding of contract negotiations, intellectual property rights, and privacy considerations, ensuring that their events operate within legal and ethical boundaries. This knowledge is essential for maintaining trust with attendees and sponsors.

Mitigating Challenges and Adapting to Trends: Challenges are inevitable in event planning, and "Influencer Events Income" prepares creators to navigate obstacles effectively. The guide explores common challenges in event organization and offers strategies for adapting to emerging trends. By staying abreast of industry shifts, influencers position themselves to create events that remain relevant and appealing to their audience.

In conclusion, "Influencer Events Income" is an invaluable resource for influencers seeking to capitalize on their digital influence and turn it into tangible income through events. By providing strategic insights, actionable advice, and a focus on ethical and engaging event execution, this e-book empowers influencers to transform their online presence into profitable ventures, showcasing the potential of influencer events in the ever-evolving landscape of digital influence.

Chapter 14

Sponsored Webinars and Takeovers Unleashed:

Elevate Your Brand Presence with Strategic Collaborations

In the ever-evolving landscape of digital marketing, sponsored webinars and takeovers have emerged as potent strategies for brands to connect with audiences in a meaningful and interactive way. "Sponsored Webinars and Takeovers Unleashed," a comprehensive e-book, serves as a definitive guide for brands and influencers seeking to harness the power of strategic collaborations through sponsored webinars and takeovers. This guide navigates the intricacies of planning, executing, and maximizing the impact of these collaborations, providing insights into audience engagement, brand visibility, and the myriad opportunities for elevating brand presence.

Understanding the Dynamics of Sponsored Webinars and Takeovers: The e-book begins by elucidating the dynamics of sponsored webinars and takeovers. It explores the distinct features of each strategy, from sponsored webinars that offer educational and interactive sessions to takeovers that involve influencers temporarily assuming control of a brand's social media accounts. Creators gain insights into the unique benefits each approach brings to brand promotion.

Strategic Collaboration Planning: At the heart of "Sponsored Webinars and Takeovers Unleashed" lies the importance of strategic collaboration planning. Brands and influencers learn to identify suitable partners, align collaboration goals, and create a roadmap for successful execution. From establishing clear objectives to defining roles and responsibilities, the guide ensures that collaborations are structured for maximum impact.

Optimizing Audience Engagement: Audience engagement is a pivotal aspect of sponsored webinars and takeovers. The guide explores strategies for capturing and maintaining audience attention throughout these interactive sessions. From crafting compelling content to integrating interactive elements such as polls and Q&A sessions, creators learn to foster a dynamic and engaging experience that resonates with the target audience.

Monetization Opportunities and Value Propositions: Monetization is a central theme, and the e-book delves into various opportunities for brands and influencers to derive value from sponsored webinars and takeovers. Creators gain insights into monetization strategies such as sponsorships, affiliate marketing, and premium access models. The guide provides a toolkit for optimizing the value proposition for sponsors and collaborators alike.

Crafting Irresistible Sponsorship Proposals: Sponsorships play a crucial role in the success of these collaborations. The e-book offers practical tips for creators to craft irresistible sponsorship proposals. From highlighting the unique value of the collaboration to showcasing the benefits for sponsors, creators gain insights into attracting lucrative partnerships that enhance the financial success of sponsored webinars and takeovers.

Leveraging Social Media Platforms: The guide emphasizes the strategic use of social media platforms for sponsored takeovers. Creators learn to leverage the unique features of platforms like Instagram, Snapchat, and TikTok to amplify brand visibility and engage with diverse audiences. From creating captivating stories to utilizing platform-specific features, influencers discover how to maximize the impact of sponsored takeovers.

Data-Driven Insights and Analytics: Data and analytics play a pivotal role in refining collaboration strategies. Creators are equipped with the knowledge to leverage analytics effectively. From tracking viewer metrics and engagement levels to analyzing conversion rates, influencers gain insights into measuring the success of sponsored webinars and takeovers, allowing for informed decisions for future collaborations.

Maintaining Brand Authenticity and Consistency: Authenticity is paramount in sponsored collaborations. The guide underscores the importance of maintaining brand authenticity and consistency throughout the collaboration. Creators learn to seamlessly integrate brand messaging into the content while preserving their unique voice, ensuring a harmonious and impactful brand presence.

Navigating Legal and Ethical Considerations: The guide addresses legal and ethical considerations inherent in sponsored collaborations. Creators gain an understanding of contract negotiations, disclosure requirements, and privacy considerations, ensuring that collaborations operate within legal and ethical boundaries. This knowledge is essential for maintaining trust with audiences and sponsors.

Mitigating Challenges and Adapting to Trends: Challenges are inherent in collaboration efforts, and the e-book prepares creators to navigate obstacles effectively. The guide explores common challenges in collaboration planning and offers strategies for adapting to emerging trends. By staying abreast of industry shifts, brands and influencers position themselves to create collaborations that remain relevant and appealing to their audience.

In conclusion, "Sponsored Webinars and Takeovers Unleashed" is a comprehensive and empowering guide for brands and influencers seeking to leverage strategic collaborations for brand elevation. By providing strategic insights, actionable advice, and a focus on ethical and engaging collaboration execution, this e-book empowers creators to transform their online presence into profitable ventures through sponsored webinars and takeovers, showcasing the potential of strategic collaborations in the dynamic landscape of digital marketing.

Chapter 15

Merchandise Magic:

Transforming Brand Loyalty into Profitable Sales

"Merchandise Magic" is an insightful e-book that serves as a guiding beacon for businesses, influencers, and content creators aiming to unlock the potential of merchandise sales as a revenue stream. This comprehensive guide navigates the intricacies of creating, promoting, and selling branded merchandise, offering valuable insights into building brand loyalty, engaging audiences, and maximizing profitability.

Understanding the Impact of Branded Merchandise: The e-book commences by highlighting the profound impact of branded merchandise in the modern business landscape. It explores how well-designed and strategically marketed merchandise not only serves as a powerful branding tool but also creates a tangible connection between a brand and its audience. Creators gain insights into the potential for merchandise to become a valuable extension of their brand identity.

Strategic Merchandise Planning and Design: At the core of "Merchandise Magic" lies the importance of strategic planning for merchandise creation. Creators learn to identify their target audience, conceptualize designs that resonate with their brand, and select high-quality products that align with their audience's preferences. The guide ensures that the merchandise reflects the brand's values, creating products that customers are eager to embrace.

Building Brand Loyalty through Merchandise: Brand loyalty is a currency of immense value, and the e-book explores how branded merchandise becomes a catalyst for fostering and reinforcing this loyalty. Creators discover how well-executed merchandise initiatives strengthen the bond with their audience, creating brand advocates who proudly showcase their affiliation through the purchase and use of branded products.

E-Commerce Platforms and Online Stores: The guide delves into the world of e-commerce platforms and online stores as pivotal avenues for merchandise sales. Creators gain insights into selecting the right platforms, optimizing product listings, and providing a seamless and secure shopping experience for customers. The e-book equips creators to leverage the digital landscape for maximum merchandise visibility and sales potential.

Strategies for Effective Merchandise Promotion: Promoting merchandise effectively is key to driving sales, and "Merchandise Magic" explores a myriad of promotional strategies. Creators learn to leverage social media, email marketing, influencer collaborations, and other channels to create buzz around their merchandise. The guide provides a toolkit for optimizing promotional efforts, ensuring that the target audience is engaged and motivated to make purchases.

Data-Driven Decision Making: Data and analytics play a pivotal role in refining merchandise strategies. Creators are equipped with the knowledge to leverage analytics effectively. From tracking sales metrics and customer demographics to analyzing conversion rates, creators gain insights into measuring the success of their merchandise initiatives and making informed decisions for future campaigns.

Monetization Beyond Product Sales: While product sales are a primary focus, "Merchandise Magic" encourages creators to explore additional monetization avenues. Creators learn about bundling strategies, limited edition releases, and exclusive merchandise for loyal customers. The e-book provides a holistic approach to merchandise monetization, ensuring a diverse and sustainable income stream.

Navigating Legal and Ethical Considerations: The guide addresses legal and ethical considerations inherent in merchandise creation and sales. Creators gain an understanding of copyright issues, trademark protection, and ethical sourcing practices. Adhering to legal standards ensures that merchandise initiatives operate within ethical boundaries and mitigates the risk of legal complications.

Mitigating Challenges and Adapting to Trends: Challenges in merchandise endeavors are inevitable, and "Merchandise Magic" prepares creators to navigate obstacles effectively. The guide explores common challenges in product sourcing, inventory management, and customer service, offering strategies for adapting to emerging trends. By staying abreast of industry shifts, creators position themselves to create merchandise initiatives that remain relevant and appealing to their audience.

In conclusion, "Merchandise Magic" is an empowering resource for businesses and creators seeking to transform brand loyalty into profitable sales through strategic merchandise initiatives. By providing actionable insights, practical advice, and a focus on ethical and engaging merchandise creation, this e-book empowers creators to establish and elevate their brand presence while maximizing profitability in the dynamic landscape of branded merchandise.

Conclusion

Unlock the full potential of social media with this comprehensive guide, designed for entrepreneurs, influencers, and businesses. From affiliate marketing and sponsored posts to product sales and coaching services, this step-by-step ebook demystifies the strategies for turning your social media presence into a profitable venture. Explore proven techniques, engage your audience authentically, and navigate the diverse avenues for revenue generation. Whether you're a novice or a seasoned social media user, this guide provides actionable insights, ethical considerations, and a roadmap for success. Elevate your online presence, build a sustainable income, and thrive in the dynamic world of social media entrepreneurship.

Thank you

www.ingramcontent.com/pod-product-compliance
Lightning Source LLC
Chambersburg PA
CBHW060835290526
45792CB00006BB/1932